ST MUNG
OF RELIGIO

GLASGOW
MUSEUMS

Chambers

Acknowledgements

We are grateful to the following for their assistance in compiling this book:
Professor Ninian Smart
Society of Friends of Glasgow Cathedral
and the staff of Glasgow Museums

The dating convention used in this book uses BCE (Before the Common Era) or CE (Common Era) which coincide with the Christian dating system BC and AD.

Front cover illustration
Christ of St John of the Cross by Salvador Dali (1904–89)

Back cover illustrations
Islamic prayer rug, 17th century
Shiva Nataraja, Hindu god, early 19th century
Lantern slide box, used by Glasgow evangelists, early 20th century

Published 1993 by W & R Chambers Ltd
43–45 Annandale Street, Edinburgh EH7 4AZ

British Library Cataloguing in Publication Data
A catalogue record for this book is available from the British Library
ISBN 0 550 22566 8

Design by James W Murray
Typeset by Buccleuch Printers Ltd, Hawick, Scotland
Printed by Bath Press Colour Books Ltd, Glasgow

Contents

PREFACE

The aim of this museum is to reflect the central importance of religion in human life. It is divided into three galleries: an Art Gallery, a Religious Life Gallery, and a Gallery of Religion in the West of Scotland.

Religion has been perhaps the single greatest inspiration to artists and craftsmen throughout human history. The Art Gallery displays objects of great beauty which communicate through art something of the meaning of the religion they represent.

The Religious Life Gallery looks at how religion pervades human life from birth, through initiation into adulthood, to marriage, through the vicissitudes of adult life, and ultimately to death and beyond.

Religion in the West of Scotland is explored in the third gallery. It tells the story of St Mungo, who is said to have founded a Christian community 1 200 years ago from which Glasgow developed. His image on the city's coat of arms symbolizes the importance Glasgow has always placed on religion. The gallery looks at how people maintain and pass on their religious beliefs and traditions, and how religions new to Scotland have come here. It also looks at missionary activities in Scotland and abroad, and at how religious communities care for the sick and the poor.

This has been an exciting and challenging museum to create. As well as reflecting the beauty inspired by religion and the worldwide diversity and pervasiveness of religious experience, the museum also demonstrates the multi-faith city Glasgow has been for at least 200 years. We have not tried to be comprehensive—this would be an impossible task, given the number of religions which exist or have existed. Instead we have drawn on our rich collections to provide a meaningful sample of the depth and variety of religious experience as reflected in objects. It is not our role to make judgements between the various religions represented here. Museums show real things, and although religion has inspired the creation of many beautiful and fascinating objects, by definition it deals with non-material beliefs and values. The museum is therefore limited to those aspects of religion which can be represented by objects. We have, however, represented world religions such as Judaism and Islam, which forbid or discourage the making of images, by displaying their written texts and items that are used for worship. Any apparent imbalance—for example in the allocation of space—simply reflects the availability of objects which are of sufficient visual interest to communicate something of importance to the visitor.

With its aesthetic, international and local perspectives this museum is unique. As far as we know, there is no museum anywhere so wide-ranging in its approach to religion. We hope that people will find it moving and rewarding.

The St Mungo Museum of Religious Life and Art owes its origins to the Society of Friends of Glasgow Cathedral. Recognizing the importance of providing facilities for the many thousands of people who come to see Glasgow's medieval cathedral every year, they decided to build a visitor centre. With initial donations from Glasgow City Council and Strathclyde Regional Council, they launched an appeal which raised a considerable sum of money from over 1 000 donors. In spite of their efforts, however, they were unable to find the money to complete and equip the building. Seeing the significance of the project, the City Council stepped in with a rescue package. This provided an opportunity for other resources within the Council to be drawn upon—specifically those of Glasgow Museums. After consider-able discussion the idea of the Museum of Religious Life and Art was born. The original intentions of the Friends will still be carried out, but in a new, worldwide context.

The museum was completed with the aid of funding provided by the Glasgow Development Agency, the European Regional Development Fund and the Scottish Tourist Board. We would like to thank them and the many others (listed in Section 6) who made contributions. We would also like to thank the many members of Glasgow's religious communities who helped by allowing us to record their feelings and beliefs about their religions and photograph their places of worship, and by donating objects. Their contribution has been crucial to making St Mungo's a living museum, reflecting not just the past but important aspects of present-day life too. With their continued participation, we hope that the museum will in some way contribute to the creation of a society better able to celebrate and respect diversity of belief.

Julian Spalding
Director
Glasgow Museums

WORLD RELIGIONS AND THEIR ART

The Ancient World

THE ANCIENT EGYPTIANS believed that the physical bodies of dead people had to be preserved, in order that their immortal spirits could survive. Bodies of royalty and wealthy people were mummified: their internal organs were first removed and the remains were then dried and wrapped in linen bandages. A MUMMY MASK [1], painted with a portrait of the dead person, was fitted over the head, and the body was placed in a coffin and finally in a tomb. The eyes on these masks were painted open so that the dead would be able to see in the after-life.

The religion of the ancient Greeks centred on a group of powerful gods and goddesses who lived on Mount Olympus but came among mortals to influence their lives and actions. The Romans adopted many of the Greek gods and their attributes, but changed their names. The legendary adventures of these gods were often depicted on art objects. The GREEK VASE [2] shows the hero Theseus, son of Aegeus, King of Athens, attacking the minotaur. The minotaur was half-man and half-bull, and lived in a labyrinth at the palace of King Minos (who was the son of the supreme Greek god Zeus and the goddess Europa) in Crete.

1. MUMMY MASK,
EGYPTIAN, ABOUT 500 BCE

2. EARTHENWARE VASE,
GREEK, ABOUT 520 BCE
(The Burrell Collection)

3. BRONZE BUST OF
HERMES, ROMAN,
1ST CENTURY CE
(The Burrell Collection)

4. GILDED LACQUER
BUDDHA SHAKYAMUNI,
BURMESE, 19TH CENTURY

5. GILT-BRONZE
BODHISATTVA
AVALOKITESVARA,
SINO-TIBETAN,
18TH CENTURY

After killing the minotaur, Theseus escaped from the labyrinth with the help of Ariadne, daughter of King Minos, and returned home to Athens. The BRONZE BUST [3] depicts Hermes, another son of Zeus. His mother was Maea, one of the daughters of Atlas (the god who was believed to support the earth on his shoulders). Hermes is best known in his role as messenger of the gods. His Roman equivalent was Mercury. This bust is a Roman copy of an earlier Greek original and was made in the first century CE.

Buddhism

Buddha, meaning 'the enlightened one', is a title that was first given to Sidharta Gautama who founded Buddhism in northern India in the sixth century BCE. For the first 400 years Buddhism represented the Buddha in symbols, such as the *stupa* (relic mound) and the *bodhi* tree, not as a person. The development of the *Mahayana* (Great Vehicle) tradition led to the worship of Buddha and other divinities or *Bodhisattvas*.

Many images of Gautama Buddha show him as a simple monk, the BUDDHA SHAKYAMUNI [4]. The serene expression on the face of this Burmese statue reflects the Buddha's approach to *Nirvana*, the release of the individual soul from reincarnation and its progress into a blissful state. The pose of this Buddha, seated on a plain lotus throne making the *mudra* (symbolic gesture) of 'calling the earth to witness', is one of the most popular images of the Buddha and refers to an event in his life just before his enlightenment. He was asked to name anyone who would give evidence that he had given alms. He moved his right hand, touched the ground, and said that the earth would bear witness that, in a previous existence, he had given so many alms that the earth had quaked.

The title Bodhisattva refers to Buddhas-to-be who have delayed reaching *Nirvana* in order to use their spiritual powers to help lesser beings. The BODHISATTVA AVALOKITESVARA [5] is the Bodhisattva of Compassion (the Chinese Guan-Yin) who took a vow that he would save all sentient beings. Later he was overcome with doubt because of the number who needed saving, and his head split into 1 000 pieces. However, the Buddha Amitabha, to whom he had made his vow, blessed him and the Bodhisattva Vajrapani offered to help. When the broken pieces of his head were reunited he became eleven-headed and looked in all directions. This Avalokitesvara stands on a lotus-flower throne which rises on a stalk from swirling waters. One of his eleven heads is missing. His many hands hold objects which represent attributes of the Buddha.

One of the most elaborate traditions in Buddhism is that of Tibet, and

9

RITUAL OBJECTS [6] play an important role in worship. Handling prayer beads helps believers memorize and repeat their *mantras* or prayers to the Buddha, and prayer wheels containing written prayers are spun. Bronze bells and skull drums are used for rhythmic emphasis during recitations of private prayer and temple ceremonies.

Christianity

Christians are followers of Jesus of Nazareth, known as Christ (which is the English equivalent—via the Greek language—of the Hebrew word *Messiah*, meaning 'the anointed one'). The story of the life and acts of Jesus is told in the New Testament, in accounts written not long after the events occurred. God chose a virgin called Mary to be the mother of Jesus, his son, who was born in a stable at Bethlehem. In 33CE, after several years of teaching, working miracles and attracting disciples, Jesus was put to death by the Roman authorities in Jerusalem.

Jesus's death by crucifixion is central to Christian belief—the Son of God who was sacrificed to save humanity from the consequences of sin (that is, from eternal damnation in Hell under the domination of Satan, God's evil adversary). Salvador Dali's CHRIST OF ST JOHN OF THE CROSS [7] was inspired by a sketch attributed to the mystic Carmelite friar St John of the Cross (1542–91). The sketch may relate to a vision of the crucifixion experienced by the friar. In this work, Dali deliberately depicted not the terrible suffering involved in Christ's ordeal, but an unblemished figure which, he felt, conveyed the ultimate beauty of God. After three days of entombment, Jesus rose from the dead. An English medieval alabaster RESURRECTION [8] depicts the actual moment when Jesus bursts out of the tomb—he is holding a triumphal banner (representing his triumph over death) and raises his right hand in a

7. *CHRIST OF ST JOHN OF THE CROSS, BY SALVADOR DALI, 1951*

gesture of blessing. Shortly after his resurrection on earth, Jesus ascended into Heaven to rejoin his father.

Before he ascended, Christ entrusted the care of his Church to his followers, who—with their successors—carried the faith into Europe. In the 11th century, after numerous differences, the Church finally split into a Western Catholic Church based in Rome and an Eastern Orthodox Church based initially in Constantinople (present-day Istanbul). In the 16th century, reform of the Western Church was initiated by Protestants, who believed that the Catholic Church was becoming corrupt and ignoring the simple nature and message of Christ's own teachings.

11

8. ALABASTER CARVING,
THE RESURRECTION,
ENGLISH, 15TH CENTURY
(The Burrell Collection)

Celebration of the *Eucharist* (also known as Mass, Holy Communion, and the Lord's Supper) is a central form of worship in the practice of the Christian religion. The service re-enacts part of Christ's last meal with his disciples, when he passed them bread and wine, saying that these were his body and blood which were to be sacrificed. Traditionally, CATHOLIC WORSHIP [9] is characterized by the use of elaborate ritual, rich vestments and precious altar equipment. These sumptuous embroidered vestments are probably Italian, and date from about 1800. The silver-gilt chalice (in which the wine is consecrated) and the silver *ciborium* (in which the Host wafers—the Body of Christ—are kept) are Spanish, and the lace chalice-cover is Italian. Rules for Catholic ritual and dress were simplified by the reforms of the Second Vatican Council (1962–5).

Icons are sacred images of Christ and major saints which play an important role in Orthodox Christianity, both in the home and in churches. CHRIST PANTOCRATOR (Ruler of the Universe) [10] shows the formal composition and subject matter found in icons, which are often painted by monks.

PROTESTANT WORSHIP [11] is in general simpler than that found in the Catholic and Orthodox traditions. Another major difference is that in some Protestant churches women can be ordained as priests; the simple black robes are those worn in 1928 by Rev Vera Kenmure, the first woman ordained to the ministry in the Congregational Union Church in Scotland. The Church of Scotland pewter communion cup and the wooden bread plate are made of humble materials, which remind believers that Jesus lived a simple life on earth and recommended others to do the same.

9. CATHOLIC WORSHIP

10. ORTHODOX ICON OF CHRIST PANTOCRATOR, PROBABLY 19TH OR 20TH CENTURY

11. PROTESTANT WORSHIP

Stained-glass windows, used in churches from medieval times, are both decorative and informative. They often illustrate biblical subjects, or depict religious figures or events from Church history. From the Old Testament, ELIJAH [12], an important Hebrew leader and prophet, is shown as he is about to be transported to Heaven by a whirlwind. God has sent a fiery chariot with horses and horsemen to fetch Elijah, who is observed by Elisha, his successor.

Saints are people who are recognized by church authorities, after their death, as having been particularly worthy Christians.

13

13. STAINED GLASS WINDOW DEPICTING
ST NICHOLAS, NETHERLANDISH,
16TH CENTURY
(The Burrell Collection)

12. STAINED GLASS WINDOW
DEPICTING ELIJAH, DESIGNED
AND MADE IN GLASGOW BY
J T AND CHARLES STEWART,
1911

ST NICHOLAS [13] was a fourth-century
bishop in what is now Turkey who,
legend relates, saved three young boys
who had been murdered, dismembered
and salted down by an innkeeper to
feed his guests during a famine.
The children are seen standing naked
in a pickling tub, while St Nicholas—
who has miraculously brought them
back to life—makes the sign of the
cross over them. In his role as patron
saint of children, St Nicholas becomes
Santa Claus, who leaves gifts for
children at Christmas time (the
birthday of Jesus).

14. Bronze Shiva Nataraja, South Indian, about 1800
15. Painted wood Krishna, Indian, 19th century

Hinduism

Hindu beliefs and practices vary from region to region in India (where the religion originated), and in areas abroad where Hindus have settled. The Hindu *Pantheon* (assembly of gods) is quite extensive and includes many important goddesses.

Shiva was originally an ancient fertility god, who was promoted to form a triad with Brahma (the creator) and Vishnu (the preserver). SHIVA AS NATARAJA (Lord of the Dance) [14] is a popular image, illustrating a legend in which Shiva subdues 10 000 heretical holy men. In the final conflict the holy men employ a fierce black dwarf, the demon of ignorance Apasmarapurusa, to destroy Shiva with a club. Shiva puts one foot on his back and performs a magical dance which is so brilliant that the dwarf and then the holy men acknowledge Shiva as their master. Shiva's whirling hair strands hold flowers, snakes, a skull and a small figure of the goddess Ganga (the holy river Ganges). The *daruma* drum in Shiva's upper right hand represents the five rhythms of manifestation (creation, preservation, destruction, embodiment and

15

release of the souls of men from illusion). The flame in his upper left hand is a symbol of the fire with which he destroys the universe. Shiva is adored by two *rishis* (sages): on his right, Patanjali (with the lower body of a snake) and on his left, Vyahrapad (who has tiger legs). The flaming halo around Shiva symbolizes the cosmos and is incised with diamonds and lotus motifs. On his forehead Shiva has a vertical *urna* (third eye).

In Hinduism, cycles of time destroy and then recreate the universe. The god Vishnu has a different incarnation in each cycle, the eighth of which is KRISHNA [15], one of the most popular gods. There are many stories of his feats, from episodes of childhood mischief to the recurrent demon-slaying battles of his maturity. These reached a peak with the battle of Kurukshetra described in the Mahabharata, before which Krishna preached the *Bhagavadgita* (Song of the Lord). The young Krishna's flute-playing charmed the married *gopis* (cowgirls), and led to an ecstatic dance of love. The romance of his courtship and marriage with one cowgirl, Radha, is celebrated in hundreds of songs and paintings. Krishna's sacred power is usually indicated by his blue or black body colour and his romances symbolize the god's love for his devotees.

DURGA [16] is the Hindu mother-goddess. Her name means 'she who is difficult to approach; the inaccessible'. Here she is shown in her fierce aspect, killing the buffalo demon Mahisha. The elephant-headed Ganesha, son of Shiva and Parvati (god of wisdom and the remover of obstacles), is also present.

Islam

It is one of the outward signs or Five Pillars of Islam that the faithful pray five times a day. Prayer takes place in private, with the community every day and on Fridays in a weekly service. The main requirement is the *quibla* (direction) to which the prayer is addressed. The person praying must face Mecca in what is now Saudi Arabia, the birthplace of the prophet Muhammad (c.570–632CE) who was chosen to propagate the religion and to whom Allah (God) revealed the Holy Book of Islam, the Qur'an. Islam has traditionally discouraged the making of images of living creatures, and its artistic traditions involve the use of geometrical and floral patterns, as seen in this 17TH CENTURY TURKISH PRAYER RUG [17]. At daybreak, noon, mid-afternoon, after sunset and early in the night a Muslim believer stands at the bottom of a prayer rug which has been positioned so that the top of the rug is pointing towards Mecca. When prostrating himself in prayer, he kneels and touches his forehead to the circular design in the arch at the top of the rug.

The word of Allah, as presented in the Qur'an, is central to Islam, and to do his message justice the text must be set down in the most beautiful handwriting possible. This led to the development of the art of calligraphy to a very high level in areas where Islam has been the main or only religion.

Judaism

The religion of the Jewish people is centred on the city of Jerusalem in Israel, site of the Temple of Solomon which was destroyed in 950BCE. The Temple contained a sacred inner sanctuary in which stood the ark of the covenant, symbol of the presence of Yahweh (God). The laws and teachings of Judaism are derived from the Hebrew Bible, which has three divisions—Law, Prophets and Writings.

The Pentateuch (first five books of the bible) includes an account of the Exodus of about 1330BCE, when Moses led the Israelites from captivity in Egypt. Passover is the important festival in the Jewish calendar which celebrates this event. At the beginning of Passover, a *Seder* meal is held, and the story of the Exodus is retold. It is unusual to find images of living creatures in Jewish art, because of a biblical prohibition, but the SEDER or PASSOVER PLATE [18] can be an exception. The words on the outer rim list elements of which *Seder* is composed,

17. ISLAMIC PRAYER RUG, TURKISH, 17TH CENTURY *(The Burrell Collection)*

18. Pewter *Seder* plate,
Bohemian, probably 17th century
(The Burrell Collection)

19. Silver filigree spice
tower made in Vienna,
1846

such as *Kadesh* (the prayer recited over the wine) and *V'rahatz* (the hand-washing) which precedes the eating of the *Karpas* (bitter herbs). Below this on the rim are depictions of the twelve tribes of Israel in animal form, alternating with circles containing the twelve signs of the Zodiac. In the centre are Moses, holding the tablets with the Ten Commandments which he had received from God, and his brother Aaron in his priestly robes. Adam and Eve, the first man and woman, are above them, and below, in another roundel, Abraham prepares to sacrifice his son Isaac when commanded to do so by God.

The Spice tower [19] is used in the Havdala ceremony, carried out on the evening of the Jewish Sabbath, which is on a Saturday and traditionally a day of complete rest. Sabbath celebrates the creation of the world by God, and the redemption of the Israelites from slavery in Egypt. Havdala marks the end of the Sabbath, and the pleasure gained from smelling aromatic spices, in addition to the renewal of light— symbolized by the lighting of a candle—helps to compensate for the prospect of beginning a new weekly cycle of work. Boxes to hold these spices have been recorded as early as the 12th century CE, but may be much older. They are made in many shapes and materials but the medieval Gothic tower is one of the most popular. Many of the prayers in the Havdala refer to God as a 'tower of salvation'.

20. KALABARI SCREEN, NIGERIAN,
PROBABLY 19TH CENTURY

21. CHIKLAT BLANKET, NORTH-WEST
COAST, AMERICAN, LATE 19TH CENTURY

The religions of small-scale societies

Many African religions involve the veneration of ancestors. Ancestors ensure the survival and welfare of the clan or extended family, usually by enforcing the continuation of customs by means of punishment, sickness or misfortune. ANCESTRAL SCREENS MADE BY THE KALABARI PEOPLE [20] commemorated the heads of trading houses, and were placed behind altars on which descendants spread offerings of food and drink for the spirit of the ancestor. The central figure is the head of the trading house; he is flanked by two sons or attendants. All possess attributes of leadership—knives, tusks and elaborate headdresses. The heads along the top of the frame probably represent slaves.

The designs on the BLANKET [21] represent animals who are held sacred as clan totems by the Chiklat division of the Tlingit people of the north-west coast of British Columbia. Such animals—which here include whales, seals, ravens, wolves and beavers—are associated with the origin and continuing welfare of specific groups of people or clans, who are usually descended from a common ancestor. The animals are portrayed in a highly stylized way using abstract fragments. The

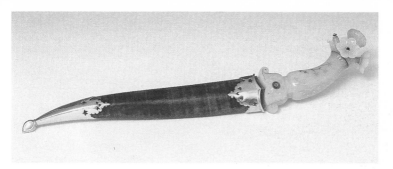

22. Sikh dagger, Indian, 19th century

blanket is woven from shredded cedar bark and mountain goat wool, and would have taken almost a year to make. Men made the looms and painted the pattern-boards from which the women copied the designs. Such blankets were highly valued up and down the coast and were worn by wealthy chiefs at important ceremonies. The most famous of these is the *potlach*, a ceremonial distribution of wealth accompanied by lavish feasting. The status of the holder was shown by his power to give, as it bound the recipients to him in a form of debt relationship. Leaders of the community would compete to give the most.

Sikhism

The Sikh religion was founded in the Punjab by Guru Nanak (1469–1539CE). Hostility from the Mogul emperors in the 17th century led to open warfare and, partly in response to this, the tenth Guru, Gobind Singh (1666–1707), instituted the Khalsa order. The *Rahit* (code of discipline) of the Khalsa includes an obligation to wear the 'Five Ks'. These are uncut hair (which is worn in a turban), breeches, an iron bangle, a comb and a dagger. This decorative version of the KHANJAR (ritual dagger) [22] has a white jade hilt carved in the shape of a lotus flower, and the steel blade has a channel containing small pearls which roll up and down when the weapon is brandished. This feature is poetically known as 'the tears of the wounded'.

Taoism

Religious Taoism emerged in China towards the end of the later Han dynasty (23–220CE). It grew out of the philosophy founded by Laozi in the sixth century BCE. He taught that 'men should not strive, but should always pursue a course of inaction because things will come to a successful conclusion without effort'. The Eight Taoist Immortals are

21

23. PORCELAIN BOWL, CHINESE, QING DYNASTY,
KANG XI PERIOD (1662–1722 CE) *(The Burrell Collection)*

legendary beings who became gods with supernatural powers as a result of doing good. The PORCELAIN BOWL [23] shows four Immortals: from left to right, Zhongli Quan (carrying the peach of longevity in both hands), Han Xiang Zi (a famous scholar and patron saint of music, carrying a flute), Li Tie Guai (an emaciated figure leaning on a crutch and carrying a gourd, representing a free spirit), and Lan Caihe (a girl carrying a basket of flowers, who is the patron saint of florists).

SECTION

2

RELIGIOUS LIFE

FROM THE REMOTEST PAST religion has pervaded daily life. It is only in relatively recent times, with the growth of industrial and scientific culture in the West and the spread of its ideas over the world, that people have attempted to live without religion. This gallery looks at some of the ways in which religion has been interwoven with many aspects of daily life: the marking of major life events such as birth, the progress to adulthood and marriage, as well as the provision of formal communal and individual prayers and ceremonies. Religion is called upon to validate rulers, inspire charitable acts, and to justify war and persecution; it inspires some to become priests, or to take up other vocational activities, and devote their whole lives to their faith. Last of all, religion helps to explain the ultimate mystery, death, and what lies beyond it.

24. EARTHENWARE PLATE, BRITISH, 19TH CENTURY

25. Bronze Isis and Horus, Egyptian, probably modern reproduction; Alabaster Virgin and Child, English, late 15th century; Porcelain Guan-Yin and child, Chinese, Qing dynasty, Kang Xi period (1662–1722 ce) *(all from The Burrell Collection)*

The Life-cycle

Birth

The beginning of life is always a momentous event. Ceremonies to mark the arrival of a new baby are often combined with initiation into the parents' religion, as in Christian baptism, or Jewish and Islamic circumcision of male babies. Other faiths postpone initiation into the faith until later.

The origin, or birth, of the human race is a mystery which most religions attempt to explain. In Judaism, Christianity and Islam, the first people created by God were Adam and Eve. On this PLATE [24] they are shown in the Garden of Eden (Paradise) beside the 'Tree of knowledge of good and evil'. Satan, in the form of a serpent, tempts Eve to taste the fruit of the tree, an act which had been forbidden by God. After Adam and Eve tasted the fruit of knowledge they were expelled from Eden. They, and all human beings since, have been tainted by the sin of disobedience and have been forced to work in order to survive. Part of Eve's punishment was the pain she and all women were to experience in childbirth.

The central importance of birth and the close relationship of mother and child have inspired powerful IMAGES OF WOMEN AND CHILDREN [25]

26. MAIOLICA BOWL, ITALIAN, ABOUT 1540

which feature in many religious contexts. The singular emotional resonance of these images over vast distances of space and time is accompanied by very different beliefs specific to the religions involved. Most religions have festivals which fall on the birthdays of their gods or their founding prophets. On the left are ISIS AND HORUS. Horus was the son of the ancient Egyptian gods Osiris and Isis, and is shown here on his mother's knee. With Osiris, Isis and Horus formed a *triad* (divine family). In the centre is a Catholic statue of the VIRGIN MARY, crowned as Queen of Heaven, with the Christchild on her arm. Images like this one were often destroyed or badly damaged during the period of the Protestant Reformation, as it was thought that Mary was the subject of worship which should be reserved only for God. On the right is GUAN-YIN, the Chinese female version of the Indian Buddhist god Avalokitesvara. The child represents all children in need of nurture. Guan-Yin is worshipped by those who desire offspring or wish their prayers to be answered.

The ITALIAN BOWL PAINTED WITH A CHILDHOOD SCENE [26] originally formed part of a set. Such sets contained plates, bowls and other eating

27. CHRISTENING GOWN, SCOTTISH, 1840s

utensils, all neatly stacked together. They were traditionally given to
women who had just given birth. Gifts to newly-born babies and their
mothers are common to many societies, and celebrate both fertility and
a safe confinement. Gifts of food or money reflect the age-old anxieties
about the survival of children—anxieties which in many countries are
still all too real.

The sacrament of baptism formally admits new members to the
Christian faith, and usually takes place at the same time that babies are
christened (given their Christian names). Baptism sometimes consists
of total immersion of the candidate, who may be a child or an adult.
This may take place in a church, or out of doors in a natural source of
water. Babies traditionally wear a CHRISTENING GOWN [27] for the
ceremony; these are often treasured as family heirlooms and worn by
babies of several generations.

Initiation

The progression from childhood to adulthood is often marked by religious rituals which may include withdrawal from everyday life, periods of fasting, tests of endurance and induction into the secrets of adult life, particularly with regard to sex. The final stage is often regarded as rebirth of the individual.

This SANDE or BUNDU SOCIETY MASK [28] from the Mende people of Sierra Leone in West Africa is worn by the leader (*Sowie*) of the *Sande*, a female society, when adolescent girls are being initiated. Through instruction in *Sande* secrets and a series of ceremonial rituals, adolescent girls become adult women. The identity of the *Sowie* is kept hidden by the mask, which would have a raffia fringe attached, and a raffia costume. The mask, which displays features common in the ideal female beauty, represents power, emotion and womanly qualities.

The initiation takes place in the bush, the neophytes being led into a special clearing, covered in a white clay wash and wearing their best clothes. They receive new *Sande* names, and the ones given at birth are discarded. The most important initiation ceremony, that of clitori-dectomy (female circumcision), takes place almost immediately. (This practice is banned by the World Health Organization, as it is far more dangerous and painful than male circumcision.) During the period of seclusion that follows, the white clay wash (partly symbolic of the

28. *SANDE* MASK, SIERRA LEONESE, 20TH CENTURY

29. MWASHAMBOY MASK, ZAIRIAN, LATE 19TH CENTURY

death of the old life) also serves to help bring down the temperature of the fever which affects most of the young women. Later the clay wash is used as a beauty treatment. Initiates are taught to be modest, hard-working and respectful to their seniors. They learn to cook, take care of the sick, and spin, weave and fish, as well as other common domestic chores. Singing and dancing are always taught, and special exhibitions of these skills are organized, culminating in the graduation ceremony. The final graduation day, when the initiates re-enter the community as adults, is a time of great rejoicing. Kendu medicine, an essential part of the *Sande* ritual, is paraded through the village by four officials. The masked *Sowie* spirit leads the girls back for a final three days' seclusion before they go on display on their parents' verandahs; shining with oil and loaded with coins and finery, seated with eyes modestly cast down, they receive the admiration and gifts which friends, suitors and relatives bring them.

The MWASHAMBOY MASK [29] dates from the late 19th century and comes from Zaire. It may be worn only by a king's son and is one of several masks used in the initiation of the Kuba, a central African people with a strong tradition of divine kingship. The mask personifies the son of Woto, the first king, mythical founder of the Kuba people and inventor of the rites. The short tail-like projection on the rear left side represents an elephant's trunk, a symbol of royal power.

Young Kuba boys spend a few days in a shelter in the village square, separated from women and uninitiated children, who are frightened away by other masked dancers. The boys enter a passage or tunnel and pass between the legs of two masqueraders, Nndup and Kalyengl, representing Woto and the mother of the spirit of Initiation. In the initiation camp they are introduced to other masks such as Yol, the policeman; Mbongakwong, a phallic mask which stresses the sexual teachings of initiation; and Mbomba, representing the political opposition of commoners. The Mwashamboy mask is also there. As the Kuba are matrilineal, the king's sons are not the royal heirs (the heir would be a son of the king's elder sister), but they are still important as royalty and have a key role in court politics.

Marriage

The relationship between men and women is one of the most powerful forces in human life. All religions provide rules for its regulation, in particular with regard to the formal union known as marriage. Depending on their religion and culture, men may have only one or more than one wife; more rarely, women may take more than one husband. The choice of partner may lie with the individuals concerned, or may be a matter for the family to arrange. Divorce, the formal ending of a marriage, may be relatively easy, difficult or impossible.

Special outfits such as this type of modern HINDU BRIDAL SUITING [30] are usually worn by participants in marriage ceremonies. Such outfits often incorporate symbolic features—traditional colours or particular accessories—which underline both the financial and the sexual importance of the ceremony in many societies. This outfit consists of a red silk *pyjama-kumeez* (a narrow-legged trouser and tunic set), with a matching georgette veil. The silk length for the suiting, made in India, is sold with the tunic front, cuffs and leg hemmings already embroidered with a dense floral design in silver and gilt threadwork.

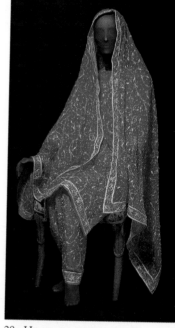

30. HINDU BRIDAL SUITING, INDIAN, LATE 20TH CENTURY

Healing

Religion and healing have always been associated. The relationship may be expressed through spiritual means such as prayers and vows, or practices such as the laying-on of hands. More direct physical treatments can involve anointing the sufferer with holy oil or water, fasting, and the taking or application of special herbs or medicines. In addition, psychological elements are often involved in the healing process; these can include confession, communal rituals of reconciliation and expressions of support.

Pilgrimage shrines often grow up around sites where healing takes place. One such shrine is at Lourdes in France, which is a favourite pilgrimage destination for Catholics. The HOLY WATER BOTTLE [31], brought back from Lourdes, was used to transport water from the spring in the Sacred Grotto where St Bernadette saw visions of the Virgin Mary in 1858. Many cures have been attested at Lourdes over the years.

31. HOLY WATER BOTTLE FROM LOURDES, 1950s

32. SPIRIT OF SMALLPOX IN CARVED, PAINTED
AND BURNED WOOD, NIGERIAN, 19TH CENTURY

33. DIVINATION CROCODILE AND CHARM
NECKLACE, CENTRAL AND WEST AFRICAN,
19TH CENTURY

Diseases were sometimes visualized, feared and respected as cult spirits. This CARVED FIGURE [32] is from the Yoruba people of Nigeria, and represents the spirit of Smallpox—one of the most destructive diseases that Europeans brought with them to Africa and the Americas.

The AFRICAN DIVINATION CROCODILE and CHARM NECKLACE [33] were both used for religious purposes. The carved crocodile with a wooden plug attached was used in Central Africa (now Zaire) in the 19th century, for divination. The plug was apparently rubbed along the crocodile's back, on which resin had been smeared; the result of the divination was dependent on whether or not the plug stuck to the surface of the wood. The charm necklace was used by a healer or medicine man. It is hung with glass beads and an assortment of West African animal parts.

Religion as a Profession

Withdrawal from everyday life to join others of like mind in monasteries or nunneries is a life path offered by many religions. Alternatives to a communal enclosed life spent in the religious profession are many; these include the options of living in solitary seclusion as a hermit or anchorite, and becoming a religious scholar or leader (such as an imam, priest, priestess or rabbi) working within society.

This statue of an ENTHRONED BUDDHIST MONK [34] shows the founder of the Lotus Flower Monastery at Sinshagshien, Chekiang, in China. He himself became the subject of veneration, as symbolized by his throne. Offerings and prayers were placed in the small recess behind the figure. In the early 20th century the monastery was converted to a Christian place of worship.

ST JEROME [35] was an Italian biblical scholar who lived around the year 400. He spent part of his life as a hermit in the Syrian desert, and he is shown here sitting at the mouth of a cave, holding the stone with which he beat his breast as penance for his sins. Legend tells that he took a thorn from the paw of a lion, who then followed him; this lion became St Jerome's attribute in art. St Jerome is best known for having translated most of the Bible from Greek into Latin (known as the

34. LACQUERED AND GILT WOODEN BUDDHIST MONK, CHINESE, 18TH CENTURY

35. MAIOLICA PLATE DEPICTING ST JEROME, ITALIAN, EARLY 16TH CENTURY

36. EARTHENWARE STATUE OF ST CLARE OF
ASSISI, MADE BY THE DELLA ROBBIA
POTTERY, BIRKENHEAD, ABOUT 1900

37. MOTHER TERESA OF CALCUTTA
(Reproduced courtesy of The Herald*)*

Vulgate version), and he wrote many learned commentaries on biblical matters.

ST CLARE OF ASSISI [36] was greatly influenced by the ideas of her friend St Francis of Assisi, who helped her set up a community of nuns in Italy in the 14th century. The community lived, like the Franciscans, according to a very strict rule of poverty. They did not possess any property at all, and existed entirely on alms (charitable donations). They eventually became known as 'Poor Clares', and still are today. St Clare is usually shown in art, as here, carrying a *monstrance*, a vessel used to display the consecrated Host; this recalls the legend of her repulsion of the Saracens' attack on Assisi by rising from her sick bed and carrying the Host to the city walls.

MOTHER TERESA OF CALCUTTA [37] is the best-known Roman Catholic nun of modern times. An Albanian, she has spent the greater part of her life tending destitute sick and dying people in the Indian city of Calcutta. Members of the order of nuns she established are found wherever there is greatest need, and are supplemented by volunteers from all over the world. Mother Teresa was awarded the Nobel Peace Prize in 1979.

Rulers

Relationships between religions and lay rulers are often complex. On the highest level, the rulers themselves are held to be divine; alternatively, the rulers may not be divine, but their rule is seen as divinely ordained and approved. Many modern societies separate totally the roles of secular and religious leaders.

This YORUBA COPE AND FLY-WHISK [38] would have been used by a chief or cult officiant in the late 19th century. The use of imported European beads was restricted to persons of importance amongst the Yoruba in Nigeria, and became a symbol of power.

In southern Nigeria, the religion of Benin includes ancestor-worship and the belief that ancestors are reincarnated in their descendants. Richly-decorated altars for ancestors of the ruling family were arranged around a courtyard; they consisted of traditional bronze vessels, figures, and heads like the MEMORIAL HEAD OF A QUEEN MOTHER [39] seen here. A large ivory tusk would have been placed vertically through the open crown of the head.

DRAGON ROBES [40] were worn by mandarins (members of the Chinese ruling élite). Such robes were mostly blue in colour, characterized by a hem design of stripes representing water, with turbulent waves above and symmetrically placed mountain peaks. On the body of the garment are dragons amidst clouds and various emblems associated with Buddhism and Taoism. These are all symbols of good fortune, and reflect the integration of state and religion up to the time of the Communist revolution. The rank of the wearer was denoted by accessories worn with the robe: a rank badge, a plain dark front-fastening surcoat, a detachable collar and, also round the neck, a string of beads. This robe was worn in Bertolucci's film *The Last Emperor*, released in 1987.

38. YORUBA COPE AND FLYWHISK, NIGERIAN, LATE 19TH CENTURY

The nine grades of rank of both civil and military mandarins were marked by square decorative badges which were attached to the front and back of the surcoat. The civil ranks were represented by various species of birds, while the military were represented by beasts. This BADGE WITH A TIGER-CAT [41] was worn by an official of the sixth rank.

39. BENIN BRONZE HEAD
OF A QUEEN MOTHER,
NIGERIAN,
EARLY 19TH CENTURY

40. DRAGON ROBE OF
EMBROIDERED SILK,
CHINESE,
LATE 19TH CENTURY

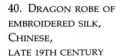

41. SILK BADGE OF RANK,
CHINESE, 19TH CENTURY

34

Missions

Christians who volunteer for missionary work abroad usually feel that they have been called upon by God to do so. Although their lives may be threatened by extreme climates, unfamiliar diseases and hostile inhabitants, they view danger and possible death as part of the task they have undertaken. As well as spreading the word of God, missionaries have usually undertaken work with a social purpose, such as teaching or nursing; the DRESS [42] shown here dates from the 1920s or 1930s and was probably worn by a missionary working as a nurse in China. The motives for this work were, in the past, both charitable and self-interested; charity is a Christian obligation, and those seen doing good naturally attracted the esteem of others, possibly inspiring them to adopt the missionary's beliefs. In many poorer countries today the practical work of missionaries is welcomed, but the religious element is sometimes seen as invasive, especially if it does not respect the culture and beliefs of the people with whom the missionaries are working.

42. MISSIONARY'S DRESS WORN IN CHINA, 1920s or 1930s

Holy Wars

Since time immemorial, wars have been justified in the name of religion. The Crusades, for example, were armed Christian expeditions undertaken to recover Jerusalem and the rest of the Holy Land from domination by the Saracens, who were Muslims. These expeditions, supported by various Popes, took place at intervals from the end of the 11th century to the middle of the 15th century. This SWORD [43] dates from about 1150, and has the letters BOAC inscribed on the blade. The letters may stand for a Latin phrase such as *Beati Omnipotentesque Armati Christi* (blessed and all-powerful armies of Christ).

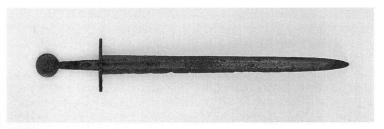

43. SWORD, CENTRAL EUROPEAN, ABOUT 1150

44. Armour worn at the Battle
of Omdurman, Sudanese, 1898

45. Earthenware statue of
St Joan of Arc,
made at Della Robbia Pottery,
Birkenhead, about 1900

The *Jihad* is an important part of Islamic belief. In general, it refers to a special spiritual effort on behalf of Allah. More specifically, it is a Holy War in defence of Islam and any soldier killed in *Jihad* will go straight to Heaven. This ARMOUR FROM OMDURMAN [44] was worn by a soldier in the army of Muhammad Ahmad, who led a rebellion (which he declared to be a *Jihad*) against the Egyptian rulers of the Sudan. He took the messianic title of *Mahdi* ('Divinely-guided one') and set up a strictly religious state in the Sudan. This lasted from 1882 until he was defeated at the Battle of Omdurman in 1898 by the Anglo-Egyptian army under Lord Kitchener.

Among unusual military leaders is ST JOAN OF ARC [45]. Also known as the 'Maid of Orleans', she was a peasant's daughter who underwent a visionary experience in which she heard voices telling her that it was her mission to save France, which was at that time at war with England. She convinced the French king of her sincerity, and led troops to relieve the city of Orleans. In 1430 she was imprisoned, sold to the English, and charged with witchcraft and heresy. She was found guilty and burned at the stake, but later declared innocent. She was made a saint in 1920. Joan's role as a military leader, and the fact that she wore men's clothes to fight in, made her a controversial figure, both in her own time and afterwards.

Death

The death of the earthly body, and what happens to the individual afterwards, is a mystery which supplies one of the greatest stimuli to the religious quest. The first evidence of human religion is found in graves of the prehistoric period. Most societies have evolved rituals for the preparation of human remains and for their disposal, safe-keeping or preservation.

Images of people who have died are often of great comfort to those left behind. This PLASTER MASK [46] was probably taken from the face of a dead child over a century ago. Before the age of photography—when many more babies and young children died than nowadays—masks like this one, or paintings, were often all that the child's parents had to help keep their memories alive.

46. PLASTER MASK OF A CHILD'S FACE, SCOTTISH, 19TH CENTURY

47. STONEWARE FIGURE OF YENLE, KING OF THE DEAD, CHINESE, MING DYNASTY, LATE 16TH TO EARLY 17TH CENTURY
(The Burrell Collection)

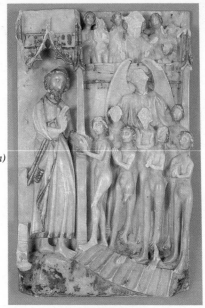

The After-life

Most religions incorporate a belief in some kind of after-life. Ancient religions, such as that of Egypt, envisaged a world where the dead would have need of useful items such as household goods, weapons and food. These goods were buried with the mummified physical remains of the dead person for his or her use in the next world.

Often, some form of judgement is involved in the process of passing from the earthly life to that which lies beyond the grave. This figure, which would have been situated in a Buddhist or Taoist temple, shows YENLE, KING OF THE DEAD [47], who ruled over the Ten Courts of Justice in the Buddhist Hell. Punishments involving torture were meted out by him and his fellow judges according to the severity of the crimes committed by the deceased. Those judged worthy would be reincarnated—each successive life conditioned by the moral value of deeds (*karma*) performed in an earlier existence. The ultimate aim is release from the endless cycle of rebirth and entry to Buddhist Paradise.

Christian belief also incorporates the concept of judgement. Since Adam and Eve tasted the forbidden fruit in the Garden of Eden they, and all human beings since, have been tempted to sin (that is, to act in ways forbidden by God). People who truly regret their sins and accept Jesus Christ as their saviour go from earth to Heaven to be with God when they die. This medieval ALABASTER CARVING [48] shows saved Christians waiting to enter Heaven. St Peter, holding the keys which represent his guardianship of Christ's Church, waits at the gate to let

49. SNAKE DEMON MASK, SRI LANKAN, PROBABLY LATE 19TH CENTURY

them in. People who do not ask Christ's forgiveness and repent their sins go to Hell—home of Satan, the embodiment of evil. This is a place where people are kept away from God forever, a punishment often represented by fire and torment.

In Hinduism, ghosts, ancestor spirits and demons often affect the living. Some demon spirits are invoked as protective countermeasures to help cure the sick. The SNAKE DEMON MASK or KOLAM NAGA RASSA [49] is from Sri Lanka. It is a traditional dance mask worn in ceremonies to drive away sickness. The bulbous eyes, long tongue and headdress with entwined and hooded cobras make a bold and dramatic representation of a *naga rassa* (snake demon). The dancers mime ancient myths in which the evil spirits causing sickness are chased away. Representations of *nagas* (snakes) existed before the development of Hindu and Buddhist imagery in South Asia, and have been incorporated in both religions. In Hinduism, they are usually demi-gods who haunt or terrorize rivers. As descendants of the sage Kayapa, the *nagas* have great spiritual strength, which may be used to combat evil. Some Hindu deities have had *avatars* (human incantations)—Vishnu is the most important example. In the other world, besides the numerous deities themselves, Buddhists and Hindus believe in the existence of *yakshas* or *yakshis* (ones worthy of worship, male or female respectively), and *asuras* (superhuman demons), as well as *nagas*. Despite belief in salvation from human existence and the wheel of rebirth, many ordinary people wish to live a long and happy life. Curative rituals harness particular spirits of the underworld to help with this.

SECTION

3

RELIGION IN THE WEST OF SCOTLAND

RELIGION HAS PLAYED A MAJOR ROLE in shaping the history, culture and identity of people in Scotland for thousands of years. Religions have changed dramatically over that time, due to incoming people— whether these were invaders, or migrants fleeing persecution or seeking a better life. The list includes Caledonians, Picts, Romans, Scots, Norsemen and, later, Irish, Jews, Italians, Lithuanians, Poles, South Asians and Chinese, all of whom brought their own religions, beliefs and traditions with them.

Change also came from within, though drawing on ideas from abroad. The reforms of Queen Margaret and her sons in the 11th century brought the church under the Roman system of bishops and dioceses. The great upheaval in European religion in the 16th century known as the Reformation took a particularly powerful form in Scotland. The Catholic Mary Queen of Scots unsuccessfully faced a challenge on two fronts: from the Calvinist reformer John Knox in her own country and from Queen Elizabeth I in England. The triumph of Protestantism was almost complete by the time Mary's son James became King of Great Britain in 1603. Religious conflict continued, however, as the Crown tried to impose the rule of bishops despite the Scottish preference for a Presbyterian system—one based on ministers. The Protestant churches in Scotland have continued the process of internal reform and renewal, responding for instance to the great changes which took place after 1780, when newly-industrialized cities such as Glasgow grew at an unprecedented pace. New or newly-aware social groups created many denominations, each striving for a more authentic adherence to the Bible, or a more just means of organizing their church.

A HIGHLAND FUNERAL [50], painted by Sir James Guthrie PRSA in 1882, highlights just one characteristic aspect of Scottish religious life. In the Highland tradition (as in the Islamic) it is a man's job to bury the dead, and only men attend funerals. The minister recites prayers over the coffin. Glasgow has a strong tie with the Highland community, and since the 18th century thousands of Highlanders (Catholic as well as Protestant) have moved to the city in search of work. Many of them still worship in churches which use their own Gaelic language.

50. *A HIGHLAND FUNERAL* BY SIR JAMES GUTHRIE, 1882

Keeping the Faith

It is a primary task of all believers to pass their religion on to the next generation and to support their fellow members in the practice of their faith. Religious practice in the home integrates religion and daily life, while most churches and other places of worship have organizations which enable their members to mix and socialize in an atmosphere conducive to the maintenance of their faith. Many of these organizations are for young people.

The BOYS' BRIGADE [51] was founded in Glasgow to promote Christian brotherhood, unity and solidarity among boys. Its organization is based on a military model, with uniforms and BANDS [52]. It encourages patriotism and loyalty to the monarchy, and is still the largest Christian organization in Scotland. The Boys' Brigade takes part, together with other youth organizations such as the Girl Guides and Brownies, in processions on Remembrance Sunday, which was established after World War I to commemorate the war dead.

Among Temperance organizations, the BAND OF HOPE [53] was the largest, aimed specifically at children and young people. The first chairman of the Scottish Band of Hope Union was William Quarrier, who was elected in 1871. He believed that it was the moral and spiritual education of children which would instil the notion of temperance and

51. THE BOYS' BRIGADE OUTSIDE THE ART GALLERY AND MUSEUM,
KELVINGROVE, UNDERNEATH THE STATUE OF ST MUNGO, 1907/8

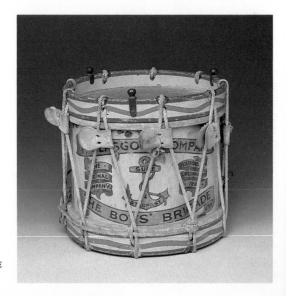

52. BOYS' BRIGADE
DRUM, 1940s

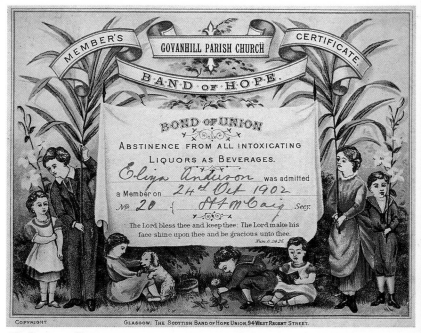

53. BAND OF HOPE PLEDGE CARD, 1902

sobriety for adult life. He also set up orphanages to house children who were abandoned or orphaned due to alcohol abuse. Past members of the Band of Hope will best remember the hymns which were sung, and the EXCURSIONS [54]. For many children, this would have been the first time they left the city to visit the seaside or the country. Today, the Band of Hope organizes talks in schools, not just about the dangers of alcohol, but the more recent threats of drug and solvent abuse.

Strict observance of the Sabbath was a feature of Scottish life after the Protestant Reformation. Church attendance was regular, and children were prohibited from playing on a Sunday unless their toys had a religious meaning. This toy, a NOAH'S ARK [55], would have recalled the account in the Old Testament of how Noah, being forewarned by God, built an ark to rescue himself, his family and a pair of each kind of animal from a great flood. Books and jigsaws on themes from the Bible were also allowed.

43

54. A Band of Hope
EXCURSION, 1920s

55. Noah's Ark toy,
19TH CENTURY

56. GARNETHILL SYNAGOGUE, GLASGOW

57. THE CENTRAL MOSQUE, GLASGOW

Immigration

GARNETHILL SYNAGOGUE [56] is the oldest synagogue still functioning in Glasgow, having been opened in 1879. It also houses the Jewish Archive, which is dedicated to recording the history of Scottish Jewry. The foundation stone was laid by Benjamin Simons in March 1877, and the building was designed by John McLeod, in cooperation with N S Joseph, a Jewish architect from London. The Jewish community in the city was formed from two waves of migration, the first fleeing Czarist persecution in Poland and Russia in the late 19th century and the second in the 1930s, fleeing Nazi persecution in Germany. Starting in the Gorbals and the city centre, the community has now moved to the suburbs of Glasgow.

Migration from South Asia to Scotland, and to Glasgow in particular, started in the early 20th century when merchant seamen from India disembarked and stayed. The main community dates from later in the century, however, when high unemployment and the great disruption caused by the partition of India and Pakistan in 1947 encouraged many to go abroad looking for a better life. The largest community is of Muslims, who established their first mosque in Glasgow in a billiard hall in Oxford Street in 1944. When the Gorbals was redeveloped, the

58. SIKH GURDWARA, GLASGOW

59. HINDU TEMPLE, GLASGOW

Oxford Street mosque was moved to Carlton Place, and then to the new CENTRAL MOSQUE [57], which opened in May 1984. This was the first purpose-built mosque in Scotland, and is one of the biggest in Europe, being able to hold 2 000 worshippers. There are also several other mosques which serve local communities in the south and west of the city.

Hindus from India mainly came here between 1947 and 1962. In the 1960s more came from the newly-independent Kenya, Malawi and Uganda, and in the 1970s many more came from the last country when all Asians were expelled. The community is served by a number of HINDU temples [58]. The Sikhs come mostly from India, and have established four GURDWARAS (Temples) [59] in the city. There are also Chinese communities who hold Buddhist, Taoist or Christian beliefs, while Scottish converts to religions such as Buddhism and Bahai'ism add to the richness of the city's religious life.

60. PARIAN WARE
STATUE OF JOHN
KNOX, POSSIBLY
MADE BY J & M P
BELL & CO,
GLASGOW,
ABOUT 1870

Reform

JOHN KNOX (1512–72) [60] was a Scottish theologian and leader of the Scottish Reformation. Trained as a Catholic priest, he encountered the ideas of the Protestant reformers first from George Wishart and later from John Calvin in Switzerland. He attacked the doctrines and corrupt practices of the Catholic Church, including its use of images and its excessive wealth. He opposed Queen Mary's attempts to restore the Catholic faith, fought with James VI over the role of bishops in the Church, and wrote many books and pamphlets.

John Ogilvie was a Jesuit missionary from Banffshire who ministered to Roman Catholics in the early 1600s. The Roman Catholic religion had been declared illegal in Scotland as a result of the Protestant Reformation of the 1560s, and Fr Ogilvie carried out his work in secret. He was betrayed to the authorities and executed at Glasgow in 1615. Every year a procession, the OGILVIE WALK [61], commemorates his martyrdom. John Ogilvie was made a saint in 1976. The first public shrine in his honour was erected in the Jesuit church of St Aloysius in Garnethill, Glasgow, and the first church to be named after him was in Easterhouse in 1957.

61. THE OGILVIE WALK IN HIGH STREET, GLASGOW, EARLY 1960s
(Reproduced courtesy of the Scottish Catholic Observer*)*

Covenanters were Christians who opposed the attempts of King
Charles I to interfere with the reformed Protestant faith. In Edinburgh
in 1638 a covenant was signed to protect the Scottish Church from his
introduction of a new English prayer book. At an assembly held in
Glasgow late in the year, the king's prayer book and other innovations
were rejected. This led to a period of bloody war and persecution for
the Covenanters. The subject of the Covenanters, who held secret
services in remote places to avoid prosecution, was a popular one for
writers (such as Thomas Carlyle) and artists during the 19th century.
THE COVENANTERS' WEDDING [62], painted by Alexander Johnstone in
1842, is one example of a painting produced at this time. It shows two
Covenanters forced to hold their marriage service in secret.

COMMUNION TOKENS [63] were used in the Church of Scotland to
organize the distribution of Holy Communion. Such a system could be
employed as a means of social control, because only people who had
been confirmed and attended church regularly would be given a token.
Today, tokens have been almost completely replaced by cards.

One of the principles introduced at the Reformation was the belief
that individuals should read the Bible in their own language, and
interpret it themselves, without need for the authority of a priest. The

49

62. *The Covenanters' Wedding* by Alexander Johnstone, 1842

63. Communion token, Scottish, c1843

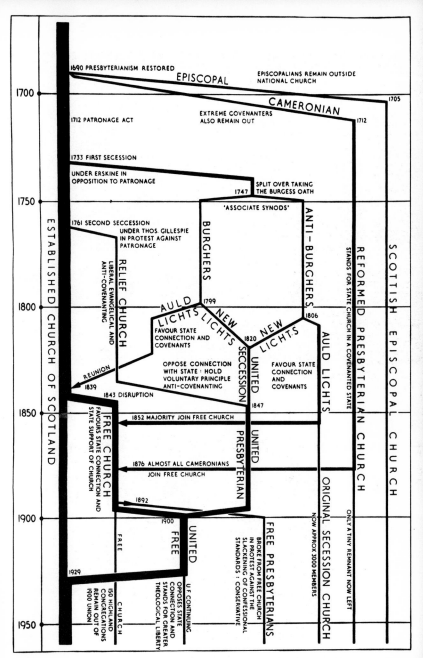

64. PROTESTANT DENOMINATIONS IN SCOTLAND (*Reproduced courtesy of
The Church History of Scotland by J H S Burleigh, Edinburgh 1988*)

65. THE DISRUPTION (*from* Annals of the Disruption, *Rev Thomas Brown, Edinburgh 1884*)

DIAGRAM OF DENOMINATIONS [64] shows how this freedom led to divisions within the new Protestant Church, sometimes over issues of doctrine but more often about how the Church related to the State.

One of the most important events in Scotland during the 19th century was THE DISRUPTION OF 1843 [65]. After almost ten years of controversy, about forty per cent of its members and more than one-third of its clergy broke away from the Church of Scotland. The causes of the controversy were the Chapel Act of 1834 which questioned whether ministers of chapels of ease (that is, churches which were extensions to the main parish churches) could take part in church courts, and the Veto Act, which gave power to a majority of male heads of families in a congregation to object to a new minister. The conservative Evangelicals, led by Thomas Chalmers, broke away in 1843 when the Court of Session repudiated the Chapel Act. The 470 ministers involved established the Free Church of Scotland. Various unions from 1847 onwards led to the Great Reunion of 1929, when most of the churches rejoined the Church of Scotland.

The Orange Order is a Protestant organization established in Ireland in 1795 to uphold the values of the Reformation. It takes its name from William, of the Dutch Royal House of Orange, who became king of the United Kingdom in 1688 and defeated the army of the Catholic King James II at the Battle of the Boyne. The Orange Order flourished in

66. ORANGE MARCH IN GLASGOW IN 1957 *(Reproduced courtesy of* The Herald*)*

Scotland from the 19th century, especially in the west, in response to the large numbers of Irish Catholic immigrants who were perceived as posing a threat to jobs and living standards. The Orange Order is run through a system of lodges, whose members organize MARCHES [66] every year to commemorate the Battle of the Boyne.

Marching and military bands featuring pipes and DRUMS [67] are an important feature of radical Protestantism in central Scotland. Orange

67. DRUM FEATURING KING
WILLIAM OF ORANGE, 1940s

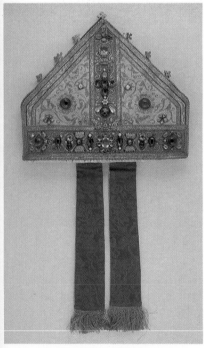

68. BISHOP'S MITRE, MADE BY
GEORGINA OLIPHANT, 1904

bands usually lead divisions of lodges of the Grand Lodge of Scotland. The main demonstration or rally in Glasgow takes place on the Saturday before 12 July each year. Many of the bands then travel to Northern Ireland to take part in marches there. On marches the bands play popular songs relating to the Battle of the Boyne, and other tunes reflecting religious divisions in both Scotland and Northern Ireland. Bands also lead church parades, when only hymns are played.

The Episcopal Church, while Protestant, retains church government by bishops (the meaning of the word *Episcopal*), as well as some of the ceremonial aspects of Roman Catholic worship. This elaborately embroidered and jewelled BISHOP'S MITRE (ceremonial headdress) [68] was made for the Episcopal Bishop of Glasgow and Galloway by Georgina Oliphant in 1904.

The movement of large numbers of Irish people to Glasgow and the west of Scotland in the 19th century led to the formation of separate communities with sympathies for each side of the conflict between Roman Catholics and Protestants in Northern Ireland, and sectarian conflict within Scotland. This MARCH IN ROYSTON ROAD, GLASGOW [69] demonstrates support for Irish republicans in Northern Ireland. Pastor Jack Glass, leading the counter-demonstration on the footpath, is the head of a small group of radical Protestants whose witness includes protesting at many ecumenical and Catholic events.

69. MARCH IN ROYSTON ROAD, GLASGOW, IN 1981
(*Reproduced courtesy of* The Herald)

The Church of Scotland is the country's official church. It grew out of the Protestant Reformation of the 1560s and was established in law by the Revolution settlement of 1690. In this, King William of Orange accepted the Presbyterian system favoured by the Scots (that is, rule by kirk sessions, presbyteries and the GENERAL ASSEMBLY [70] rather than by bishops). The General Assembly meets every year in Edinburgh to discuss matters relating to the local presbyteries as well as national concerns. The monarch, as head of the Church, is represented by the High Commissioner, and a Moderator is appointed each year to preside at the meeting and represent the Church at a number of ceremonial occasions in the ensuing year.

Missions and Temperance

The Temperance Movement was founded in Glasgow in 1829 by John Dunlop, a Maryhill philanthropist. He was concerned about the morals of the Scottish people, which he compared unfavourably with Catholic France, and which he believed were made worse by heavy drinking. The aim of the Temperance Movement was to foster abstinence from alcohol, which was a major cause of criminal activity, family violence and spendthrift behaviour. The movement was supported by William

70. THE GENERAL ASSEMBLY OF THE CHURCH OF SCOTLAND, 1981

Collins, a Glasgow printer who published many pamphlets on the subject, such as the TEMPERANCE PENNY MAGAZINE [71].

This POSTER [72] advertises the visit to Glasgow of the militant American Temperance preacher CARRIE NATION [73] in 1908. Her hostility to alcohol was so great that she believed that it was legitimate for women to kill those who offered it to their sons. She carried a Bible, and an axe which she used to smash bars in public houses.

The Salvation Army was founded in London by William Booth in 1878 and came to Scotland in 1879. It is organized on military lines, and uses uniforms and bands in its evangelical meetings. These are held in citadels or in the open air, wherever they may reach potential converts. The Salvation Army's motto is 'Blood and Fire', evoking the redeeming blood of Christ and the renewing fire of the Holy Spirit. The colours of the FLAG [74] also have symbolic meanings: red for the blood of Christ, blue for God the Father and yellow for the fire of the Holy Spirit. In the 1980s the Scottish Division was absorbed into the British headquarters. As well as preaching, the Salvation Army has always been involved in social work. Hostels are provided for homeless people and meals for the poor. Money for these activities is raised by selling furniture and other goods donated by the public.

71. An illustration from *The Temperance Penny Magazine*, 1836

72. Poster promoting the visit of Carrie Nation, 1908

73. SILVER AND MOTHER-OF-PEARL BROOCH COMMEMORATING THE VISIT OF CARRIE NATION TO GLASGOW, 1908

74. SALVATION ARMY FLAG, MODERN

75. TOM HONEYMAN

76. LANTERN SLIDE, BRITISH, LATE 19TH CENTURY

The Independent Order of Good Templars was a worldwide temperance organization which came to Scotland in 1869 and grew very rapidly. Scotland eventually had the largest lodges in the world, the record being held by that at Airdrie, with 4198 members. The Order took its name from the Knights Templar, a religious military organization set up in the 12th century to protect pilgrims visiting the Holy Land. It used elaborate regalia, ranging from sashes to processional banners, many of which exhibited biblical symbols. TOM HONEYMAN (1858–1934) [75] was international secretary for over twenty years, and edited and published *The International Good Templar* quarterly magazine.

This LANTERN SLIDE [76] is the first of a series which was shown in evangelical meetings throughout Britain in the late 19th century. The story concerns a man who only has enough money for either a pint of beer or a bowl of cherries. It continues to show the degradation of himself and his family if he buys the beer, and the improvement in their life if he buys the cherries.

BESSIE SYKES [77], who died in 1982, was one of the best-loved evangelists in Glasgow. With her husband SETH [78] she set up mission halls, distributed literature and conducted open-air meetings, mostly in the north of the city. Bessie played a portable organ and led the public

77. BESSIE SYKES

FROM
Glasgow Tramcar to Gospel Platform.

The Testimony of Evangelist Seth Sykes.

78. SETH SYKES

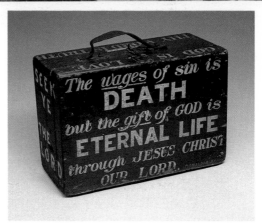

79. LANTERN SLIDE
BOX USED BY BESSIE
AND SETH SYKES

80. BILLY GRAHAM IN CELTIC PARK, GLASGOW, 1991

in rousing Gospel choruses, many of which she composed herself. The most famous of these was 'Love, wonderful love'. After Seth's death she continued their missionary work alone, and showed slides of her husband's life as an example of the transforming effect of Christian faith. The Sykeses carried their lantern slides around in this special BOX [79].

Billy Graham, the world-famous American evangelist, has visited Glasgow many times and led two major Christian missions here in 1955 and 1991. He communicates directly with people from different strands of Christianity at large public meetings. Attendances at the 1991 CRUSADE [80] were lower than those in 1955 (when a total of 830 000 heard him preach), but were still significant.

81. THE PAPAL MASS IN BELLAHOUSTON PARK, GLASGOW, 1982
(*Reproduced courtesy of the* Scottish Catholic Observer)

Pope John Paul II was the first pope to visit Scotland, and to celebrate Mass here, in June 1982. At the MASS IN BELLAHOUSTON PARK, GLASGOW [81] over 270 000 Roman Catholics and other Christians heard him praise the witness of the Catholic Church in Scotland. The papal visit provided the Church with an opportunity of strengthening the beliefs of the faithful, and of encouraging lapsed Catholics to return to the practice of their faith.

Charity

In 1414 a law was passed in Scotland forcing all beggars to be restricted to specific parishes and towns. They were later forced to get legal permission and wear BADGES [82] in order to beg. A change in attitude to the poor had occurred, associated with the Protestant Reformation and the emerging capitalist economy. The traditional obligation of CHARITY TOWARDS THE POOR [83] did not, the 1560 Book of Discipline emphasized, include the 'stout and strong beggar', but only the 'widow and fatherless, the aged, impotent or lamed, who neither can nor may travail for their sustenation'. The able-bodied poor were to be forced to work, or to return to their own parish.

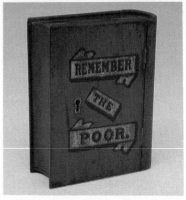

82. BEGGARS' BADGES,
18TH CENTURY

83. COLLECTING BOX,
LATE 19TH CENTURY

JOHN WHEATLEY (1869–1930) [84] was an Irish Catholic who came to Glasgow with his family when he was nine. He worked as a coal miner from the age of 11 to 24, when his self-education enabled him to pursue other jobs, ultimately as a successful journalist, printer and publisher. He became a leading figure in Scottish socialist circles, and argued that it was possible to be both a Catholic and a socialist. At first he received opposition from the Catholic Union of the Archdiocese of Glasgow, which expressed the views of the Church on secular affairs. The Church feared both socialism and secularism. In 1906 Wheatly formed the Catholic Socialist Society. He was involved in the Rent Strike of 1915 and the activities of the Red Clydesiders after World War I. He was elected to parliament in 1922, becoming Minister for Health in the first Labour government in 1924. The acceptance by the Catholic Church that Labour was not necessarily a godless creed contributed to the party's dominance of Glasgow politics after 1933.

84. BRONZE BUST OF JOHN WHEATLEY
BY A PROUDFOOT, 1934

SECTION

4

ST MUNGO

S T MUNGO [85], sometimes known as St Kentigern, is the patron
saint of Glasgow, believed to be the first person to establish the
Christian faith in the area. There are very few reliable stories about his
life or the small religious community which he established on the site of
the present cathedral. The most complete extant life of the saint was
compiled by Jocelyn, a monk at Furness Abbey in Lancashire, but this
was written five centuries after Mungo's death. In the tradition of
medieval biographers, fact and fiction are intertwined, for the Life was
commissioned at a time when Glasgow was rising as an important
ecclesiastical town and conscious efforts were made to glorify the
town's traditional founder.

The legend of St Mungo relates how his mother, St Thenog, was
raped by a pagan prince and banished by her father when she was
found to be pregnant. After the failure of various attempts to kill her,
she was placed in a small coracle without oars and cast into the Firth of
Forth. The story tells how the boat was guided by a shoal of fish until it
landed on the shores of Fife near Culross. Thenog gave birth to Mungo
on the seashore, a spot still marked by a ruined chapel. They were
taken into the care of St Serf, the head of a nearby Celtic monastic
community. There Mungo grew up and received his training as a
priest. The name 'Mungo', meaning 'dear one', was given to him by St
Serf, on account of their close friendship.

Mungo established a small monastic community on the slopes of the
Molindinar, a tributary of the River Clyde. He was later chosen to be
bishop of the area by the king and his people. Mungo died on
13 January 603 and was buried in a grave, the site of which is now
occupied by the Cathedral.

GLASGOW CATHEDRAL

The CATHEDRAL which stands today [86] was built largely between the
13th and 14th centuries. It is one of the finest examples of Gothic
architecture in Scotland, and is the largest cathedral after St Andrews
Cathedral in Fife. The seat of the Bishops of Glasgow, it also contained
the shrine of St Mungo, which became a famous place of pilgrimage
during the Middle Ages.

85. STATUETTE OF ST MUNGO,
MADE FROM OAK FROM THE
CATHEDRAL ROOF, MODERN

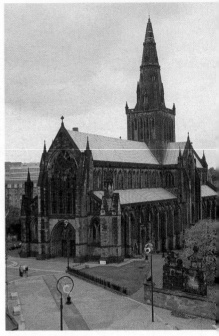

86. GLASGOW CATHEDRAL

The first permanent stone church erected over Mungo's grave was consecrated in 1136 in the presence of King David I. After it was destroyed by fire, a second church was built in 1197 by Bishop Jocelyn (1175–99), parts of which can be seen in the Lower Church of the present building.

The present Cathedral contains certain features which are unique, most notably, the magnificent Lower Church beneath the Choir and Eastern Chapels, completed during the episcopate of William de Bondington (1233–58). The Lower Church also contains the site of the original BURIAL PLACE OF ST MUNGO, situated amidst a forest of gothic vaults and columns [87]. At some point, probably in the 12th century, his bones were taken up and enshrined behind the High Altar of the Choir in the Upper Church. The original stone base of St Mungo's shrine can be seen in the Lower Church.

In the Middle Ages the Cathedral glowed with colour. Altars and reredoses were fixed against the pillars of the NAVE, imitating European models. Many of these altars were endowed by craft guilds, such as the stonemasons and the skinners [88]. The last great additions to the fabric of the Cathedral were made at the beginning of the 16th century. These included the elaborate ribbed vault in the Blackadder Aisle and the stone altar platforms at the entrance to the Choir, added by Robert Blackadder (1483–1508), who became the first Archbishop of Glasgow in 1492.

87. THE SITE OF THE TOMB OF ST MUNGO, GLASGOW CATHEDRAL

88. Glasgow Cathedral, looking east.

THE REFORMATION AND
ITS AFTERMATH

Like other churches in Scotland, the cathedral fell victim to the destruction and iconoclasm of the Protestant Reformers of the late 16th century. All images, paintings, glass and 'relicks of popery' were destroyed, and only a few of the cathedral's treasures were smuggled abroad by James Beaton, the last of the medieval archbishops. The destruction was so thorough that the only pre-Reformation image of St Mungo left is in Cologne Cathedral, Germany.

In the next century, the Cathedral witnessed struggles between Presbyterian and Episcopal forms of worship. One of the most critical General Assemblies of the Church was held in the nave in 1638. At this Assembly, the anglicizing reforms of the High Church by King Charles I were abolished, heralding a bitter war between Covenanters and Royalists. The matter was finally concluded when Presbyterianism was declared the established church in the settlement of 1690.

After the Reformation the Cathedral was split into three separate churches, each used by different congregations. This arrangement

lasted until 1805, when the last congregation left to form the Barony Church on Cathedral Square. In the 1840s the two western medieval towers were demolished in preparation for a grand restoration scheme. Fortunately, this scheme—which would have inflicted irreparable damage to the character of the building—was abandoned, due to lack of finances.

THE CATHEDRAL TODAY

In the present century much has been done to enhance the beauty of the Cathedral fabric. Under the munificence of the Society of Friends of Glasgow Cathedral, founded by Rev Neville Davidson in 1938, stained glass, chapel furnishings and fittings have been added, accentuating the medieval atmosphere of the building. The building is the responsibility of a government agency (Historic Scotland) but is still used for regular Sunday worship. The Cathedral is regarded as the mother church of the city, and as such is the venue for events of local and national significance. For example, the Cathedral was chosen as the venue for the National Thanksgiving Service for the end of the Gulf War in 1991. The service was attended by Her Majesty the Queen, the Prime Minister and the Cabinet.

THE CATHEDRAL PRECINCT

In the Middle Ages, the area around the Cathedral formed the nucleus of civil and ecclesiastical government. Glasgow was erected as a Burgh of Barony by King William the Lion in 1175, placing the administration of the town on the bishop and his chosen magistrates. Grouped around the precinct were the prebendal manses of the cathedral canons, who were responsible for serving the church. The thirty-two canons who made up the Cathedral chapter lived for part of the time in these manses and part of the time in their respective parishes round the Diocese. The manse of the Prebend of Provan still stands, known today as PROVAND'S LORDSHIP [89]. This plain, crow-stepped building of three storeys was built in 1471 by Bishop Andrew Muirhead as the clergy house of St Nicholas's Hospital. Today this building is administered by Glasgow Museums and contains period rooms and domestic furniture, mostly from the 17th century.

90. ETCHING OF THE BISHOPS' CASTLE, SHOWING THE NOW-DEMOLISHED TOWERS OF THE CATHEDRAL, 19TH CENTURY

THE BISHOP'S CASTLE

The St Mungo Museum and Cathedral Visitor Centre occupy the site of the medieval CASTLE OF THE BISHOPS OF GLASGOW [90]. Records of a castle on the site go back to 1258. It was surrounded by a high wall, attached to which was the tower of Archbishop Beaton (1508–23). Inside was the Z-shaped castle, the central tower of which displayed the arms of Bishop Cameron (1426–46). The castle contained a hall and a small chapel for the private use of the bishops. After the Reformation it was used by Protestant archbishops until the final overthrow of episcopacy in 1688. By the 1720s the castle was in ruins; it was finally demolished in 1792. The Royal Infirmary, opened in 1792, was built on the northern end of the castle site.

SECTION

5

HOW TO FIND OUT MORE

Brown, Callum: *The Social History of Religion in Scotland since 1730* (Methuen, London, 1987)

Donnachie, I and Hewitt, G: *A Companion to Scottish History* (B T Batsford Ltd, London, 1989)

Goring, Rosemary (ed.): *Chambers Dictionary of Beliefs and Religions* (Chambers, Edinburgh, 1992)

Hinnels, J R (ed.): *The Penguin Dictionary of Religions* (Penguin, Hardmondsworth, 1984)

Maan, Bashir: *The New Scots, The Story of Asians in Scotland* (John Donald Publishers Ltd, Edinburgh, 1992)

Morris, J W: *A Walk through Glasgow Cathedral* (Society of Friends of Glasgow Cathedral, Glasgow, 1988)

Smart, Ninian: *The World's Religions* (Cambridge University Press, Cambridge, 1989)

SECTION
6

*Glasgow City Council and the Society of Friends of Glasgow Cathedral thank
the following organizations and individuals who generously contributed
towards the building and development of the* St Mungo Museum
and Cathedral Visitor Centre.

PATRONS

The BP Group of Companies in Scotland · Bank of Scotland
D W T Cargill Fund · The W A Cargill Charitable Trust
Clydesdale Bank PLC · Mr John W Fleming
The Hugh Fraser Foundation · Glasgow City Council
The Glasgow Dean of Guild Court Trust
The Merchants House of Glasgow · Page & Park Architects
The Robertson Trust · The Royal Bank of Scotland plc
The Russell Lang Charitable Trust · Scottish Mutual Assurance
The Society of Friends of Glasgow Cathedral · Cathedral Congregation
Cathedral Ladies Association · STAR Foundation
Strathclyde Regional Council · TSB Bank Scotland plc
TSB Foundation for Scotland · Wm Teacher & Sons Ltd
Tennent Caledonian Breweries Ltd · The Trades House of Glasgow
Truth Research Foundation

AMW Charitable Trust · Abbey National PLC
Arthur Andersen · Arbor Ltd · Arbuckle Smith & Co Ltd
Argyll Group PLC · The Baird Trust · The Balure Trust
Barclay & Mathieson Ltd · Barclays Bank PLC
Barr & Stroud Ltd · Barr & Wray Ltd
Robert Barr's Charitable Trust
Bellahouston Bequest Fund · Blyth & Blyth Service Co Ltd
Bone, Connell & Baxters Ltd · The Boyd Trust · Bulten Ltd
The Burns Club of London · Caledonian Society
Malcolm Campbell Limited · Carntyne Electronics Ltd
Cathedral Mission · The Cathedral Sunday School
Chivas Brothers Limited · City of Glasgow Friendly Society
City of Glasgow Society of Social Service
Wm Clark Stephen Ltd · Clyde Shipping Co Ltd
Clydeport Limited · Coats Viyella PLC · D & H Cohen Ltd
Comprehensive Design Group
Martin Connell Charitable Trust
Cookson Industrial Materials Ltd

Mr L I R Abbott · Miss Ivy Aitchison · Miss E Aitken · Mr & Mrs R O Aitken
Mr Armstrong Alison · Miss M Allan · Mr & Mrs A Anderson
Mr Brian R Anderson · Mr & Mrs E Anderson · Mr & Mrs J Anderson
Mr John N Anderson · Miss R Anderson · Mr & Mrs R Anderson
Mr D d'Angelo · Mrs J Angus · Mr & Mrs John C Annan · Mr David C Ayers
Mr Alex F Baillie · Mr D Baillie · Miss J B G Baird · Mrs Mary E Baird
Mr Henry W Baker · Prof & Mrs Neville Baker · Mr John Balding
Miss M H Barclay · Miss Olive Barclay · Mr & Mrs R H Barclay
Mr Stuart Lothian Barclay · Rev David Barr · Mr George G Beck
Mr W K Begg obe · Mr Christopher M Bell · Mrs Margaret J Bell · Ms V E Bell
Mr & Mrs William Bell · Mr Adam Berry · Mrs Muriel Bett · Mr Donald Black
Miss E M Black · Mrs P Black · Mr Scott A Black · Miss S C H Blair
Dr & Mrs W Blair · Mrs Eva M Blanche · Mrs Alice S K Bolton · Miss C C Bone
Mrs & Mrs S Boshell · Mr William Bowie · Prof & Mrs William C Bowman
Mr & Mrs J Boyack · Dr & Mrs Gavin Boyd · Miss Mary L Boyd
Mrs G & Miss M Boyes · Mr & Mrs R C Brechin · Mr John H D Bridges
Mr A Brock · Miss A A Brock · Miss M Brock · Mr R Brock
Mr Charles Sutherland Brown · Miss Helen C Brown · Miss I O R Brown
Mr James A Brown · Mr W Brown · Mr & Mrs Eric Bryson
Mr Robert G Bryson · Alison M Buchanan · Miss Doris Buchanan
Miss Eileen Buchanan · Dr Marjory M Buchanan · Mr I Burns
Miss C Burnside · Miss Jean Cadzow · Mr John Cairnduff · Mrs E M Cairnie
Mr Douglas Caldwell · Jack & Doreen Caldwell
Misses M A & J T H Callaghan · Ms H Frances Cameron · Mr Alex Campbell
Miss H Hope Campbell · Mr James Dawson Campbell
Mr & Mrs Kenneth Campbell · Dr M W Menzies Campbell · Mr Neil L Campbell
Mrs E M Carmichael · Mrs E P Carmichael · Mr J F Carnegie
Major General & Mrs T W Carrick · Miss M Carruthers
Mr William A Carruthers · Mr James N Carstairs · Mr John M Caskie
Miss Elizabeth S F Cassells · Miss June E Caunce · Mr & Mrs Peter Chalmers
Dr R S Chapman · Miss Norma Christie · Mr Robert Church · Dr John Clark
Lord & Lady Clydesmuir · Dr David J Coats · Mrs Lily Cochrane
Mrs D M K Collie · Mr & Mrs Glen Collie · Mrs Annie Colquhoun
Miss M Connell · Drs Hugh & Lilian Conway · Mrs J Couper
Mr Alan M Coutts · Mr Ian James Cowan · Miss K M Cowan
Mr William P H Cowan · Mrs Agnes Craib · Miss A Craig
Mr Thomas R Craig cbe · Miss Sheila M Craik · Mr & Mrs J P Cranston
Mr Maurice Crichton · Mr Diarmid A Cross · Baroness of Culcreuch
Miss P A T Cullen · Mr Arthur F Cumming · Miss Christina S Cunningham
Mr & Mrs R F C Cunningham · Mrs W Cunningham
Sir Samuel Curran dl feng frs · Mrs & Mrs J Currie · Mr Alan Cuthbert
Miss G R Cuthbert · Mr William Moncrieff Cuthbert · Miss Muriel G Cuthill
Mr James Wadell Dallachy · Miss M M Dare · Mr John A Davidson
Mr & Mrs I Dawes · Mrs G A Deans · Miss Violet M Denholm

Mr George D H Dewar · Mr Tom Dewar · Mr & Mrs A Diack
Miss Agnes Dickson · Mrs G Y Dickson · Mrs J Dickson · Ms Ann Doak
Mrs P A Doig · Miss Susan Dolan · Rev Thomas & Mrs M E Donald
Mr Robert Douglas · Mr & Mrs D B Downie · Mrs Una Downs
Miss C Drummond · Mr Morrison Dunbar · Mrs I S Duncan
Mr Robert J Dunlop · Mrs Irene C Dunn · Dr Helen S Dunsmore
Mr Ian L Dunsmore · Miss Charlotte Duthie · Miss Margaret Dykes
Miss Agnes S Eddie · Mr & Mrs M Eden-Bushell · Rev Albert B Elder
Mr Robert Elliot · The Rt Hon Baroness Elliot of Harwood · Mr J Emmerson
Mr Michael Charles Everist · Miss Jean Ewen · Mr & Mrs R Ewing
Rev Ian C M Fairweather ma bd & Mrs Joan Fairweather ma
Mr & Mrs W R J Fairweather · Mr & Mrs Derek F Fearn · Mr Joseph Fell
Mrs Maysie M Fenton · Mr & Mrs T Fergus · Mr J M Ferguson
Mrs Margaret J Ferguson · Mrs Mary Ferguson
Miss Rachel Kennedy Ferguson · Mr F Findlay · Mrs J B Findlay
Mrs N S Finlay · Dr I Finlayson · Rev James Finlayson
Mr Alan James Fitzpatrick · Mr & Mrs S G Fleck · Miss Jean Fleming
Mr Leslie Drummond Fleming · Mr Peter Fleming-Brown
Mr & Mrs Alex Fletcher · Mr Donald L M Forbes · Miss E Forrest
Dr D A R Forrester · Mrs Marion W Forrester · Cdr & Mrs A M Fraser
Mr Gordon S Frier · Miss Muriel Irene Fulton · Mr & Mrs J P Fyfe
Mrs Jean Galbraith · Mrs Amy Galloway · Mr George Galloway
Miss J Galloway · Ms B Gardiner · Mr George G P Gardiner · Mr L Gardner
Brian & Lorna Garthwaite · Miss L A Gedd · Mr Michael C Gellatly
Miss M A Gemmell · Mr William F Gemmell ca · Mr John Gerrard
Mr & Mrs Nigel Dewar Gibb · Mrs Alison S Gifford · Ms M Gilchrist
Mrs J Gillespie · Mr A Barclay Gilmour · Mr Robin Moffat Gilmour
G S Gimson qc · Mrs Sheena Glass · Mr & Mrs E Glen · Mr John Glover
Ms Jane Goldie · Mr W N Gordon · Mrs J Gorman · Mrs M M Gracie
Prof N B Graham bsc phd cchem frsc fpri · Mr W Alex Graham · A Grant
Mrs C P C Grant · Dr Charles P Grant · Mr Ian H Grant
Mrs Margaret J Y Grant da · Mrs Richard Grant-Rennick · Mr David Gray
Mr John R Gray · Mr Thomas Gray · Sir William Gray · Mary Grierson
Col & Mrs J F Kerr Grieve · Rev & Mrs A F Grimstone · Mr Graham W Guthrie
Marion & Andrew Haberman · Mrs A Haggerty · Miss H Hales
Mrs Nanette Hales · Prof & Mrs J M Halliday · Mr & Mrs A F Hamilton
Mrs Jean Hamilton · Mrs Margaret G Hamilton · Mrs Mae M Hardy
Mr Kristopher D Harrower · Mr & Mrs John M Harvey · Mrs M Harvey
Mr & Mrs John S Harvie · Mr Robert Hastings · Miss Isobel M Hay
Edith Lady Headley · Dr J Hely · Mr A D R Henderson · Audrey Henderson
Mrs Helen Henderson · Mrs J Henderson · Mr A Brodie Hepburn
Mr & Mrs J Hepburn · Mr Gavin Hercus · Miss M Herd · Mrs C Hewitt
Mr Walter O Hibberd · Mrs R Hilley · Dr & Mrs G J Hills
Mr & Mrs James Kerr Hiorns · Sir Michael & Lady Hirst · Mr A G Hodge

Mr S Graham Hoey · Mrs Hope Hogg · Mr Archibald L Holmes MBE
Mrs I Holmes · The Rt Hon Lord Home KT PC · Mr W J Horne
Mrs E R Houston · Mrs H Y Houston · Ms Janet M S Houstoun
Mr James T Howat · Miss M Howatson · Miss K Howe · Miss Rachel Howie
Mrs P Hughes · Mr Neil Hughes-Onslow · Mr J D H Hume
Mrs Ailene S Hunter · Miss M F Hunter · Mr William H Hunter
Mrs Noreen Hurll · Miss Romena Huq · Dr & Mrs R T Hutcheson
Prof James H Hutchison · Mrs M Irwin · Mr W Alastair Jack
Dr W A P Jack CBE DUNIV KSTJ FRIBA FSA(SCOT) · Mrs Helen P Jerdan
Mr Roy A Johnson · Mr Ivor S Johnston · Mrs J Johnston
Mrs Jane Johnston · Mrs Elizabeth B C Johnstone · Miss J Johnstone
Mrs G Jones · Mr Owen D Jolly · Mr R Keir-Watson · Mrs Christina A Kelly
Mr & Mrs J M Kempsell · Mrs Olive E Kerr · Mr John M Kier
Mr & Mrs H A Kingcome · Miss Edith Kinnear · Mr J Knox · Miss Theo Kwansa
Mrs F M Laird · Mrs W Lamont · Mr & Mrs Ron Lander
Mr J R Lang CBE MI MECHE · Mrs V Langston · Miss E Law · Mrs Muriel Law
Mr Harry Lawd III · Mr Neil M Lawrence · Mrs C G Lawrie
Miss Alice W Lawson · Mr Andrew Lawson KSTJ JP DL · Mr W U P Lawson CA
Mr G Alastair Lean OBE · Miss E Lee · Miss Marilyn Lees · Mrs Olive Lees
Miss Victoria M M Lees · Mrs J Leggat · Rev E M H Lewis · Mr Gavin Lightbody
Mr & Mrs Gordon A Lightbody · Mr James Lightbody · Mrs Barbara G D Linn
Miss Elizabeth Liversidge MBE · Miss E C Livingstone
Mrs Elizabeth W Lochhead · Miss Helen I Logan · Mr Jimmy Logan
Mr & Mrs R Logan · Miss Ann M Loudon · Mr James Pope Loudon
Mr Neill Loughty · Mr & Mrs John R Lundie · Rev J C & Mrs I M Lusk
Mr Ian Lyall CBE · Mrs E S Lyle · Miss Janet W Lyle · Mr John M Lyle
Mr Graham W A MacAllister · Dr Irene M McAlpine · Mrs Moira MacAskill
Dr James Macaulay · Ms Mary McCabe · Mrs Maggie McCaig
Mr J A G McCall · G Jean McCallum · Mr Hugh S McCallum · Miss C C McCaw
Mr G M A McChlery · Mr & Mrs R McClinton · Mr John McCormick
Mr Alister G McCrae CBE · Miss Grace M McCrone · Mr Thomas McCubbin CA
Mr & Mrs Frank McCue · Mr George McCulloch
Mrs Anne Maxwell MacDonald · Miss C MacDonald · Miss C A MacDonald
Mr John MacDonald · Miss M Macdonald · Mr N MacDonald
Mr Norman MacDonald · Miss Shiela T McDonald
Mr Angus M MacDougall · Miss Marie McDougall · Eleanor McDowall
Mr & Mrs W R McElroy · Mr John McFarlan · Lord Macfarlane of Bearsden
Mrs Marie Macfarlane · Mr L B McGibbon · Mr W P McGowan
Mr & Mrs W McGrath · Miss Agnes McGraw · Mr W Lawrie Macharg
Mr James McHugh · Mr A E McIlwain CBE · Misses Shona & Wendy McIlwain
Miss Mary McIlwraith · Mrs Ellen C Mcintosh · Mr James McKeand
Mr Henry McKechnie · Mr C D R McKellar · Mrs S McKendry
Rev Lindsay McKenna · Mr & Mrs R O MacKenna · Miss F R Mackenzie
Mr J Mackenzie · Mr L R N Mackenzie · Miss M E Mackenzie

Mr Douglas G McKerrell · Miss Mary C Mackie
Mr David & Mrs Gillian Mackilligin · Dr & Mrs G C McKinlay
Mr & Mrs B McLaren · Mr & Mrs A J McLay · Mr J McLay · Mr & Mrs J McLay
Mr C Hector MacLean · Miss Elizabeth A McLellan · Mrs J McLellan
Sir Robin MacLellan · Mr James F McLelland · Mr James C MacLeod
Mrs Anne McLuskey · Miss Susan McLuskey · Miss Ann McMillan
Mrs M McMillan · Mr Norman W McMillan · Miss Catherine C McMurtrie
Mr Douglas M McNicol · Mr Colin S McPhail · Mr & Mrs J MacRae
Mr & Mrs James MacShannon · Dr Alison E Mack · Mrs Helen F Mack
Mr & Mrs R W Mackin · Miss Anne F Mair · Dr & Mrs Robert D Mairs
Mr Kenneth G Manley · Mr A R H Mann · Miss C Marchbank
Mr R D Margetts · Mr James Marshall · Mr & Mrs J Marshall
Mrs E B G Martin · Mr James W Mason · Mr & Mrs John N C Mason
Mr & Mrs K W Mason · Mrs Marjory C Mason · Mrs Marjorie G Matheson
Mr & Mrs D Matthew · Mr H A Mavor · Mr J O Mavor · Miss Moira Meighan
Mr James S D Meikle · Mr & Mrs P J Methven · Mr John Mill
Rev J Stuart Mill & Mrs Mill · Mrs D H Millar & Mr J Millar · Miss F Miller
Mrs M Murray Miller · Miss P R Miller · Mr & Mrs S Miller
Rev Archibald H Minto · Mr J Mitchell · Miss Agnes Morris · Mrs D Morris
Mr D W H Morris · Miss Margaret S Morris
The Very Rev Dr Wm J Morris & Mrs Jean Morris cbe · Mr B L Morrison
Mr E S M Morrison · Miss Lilias S Morrison · Elizabeth G Morton
Mr M Mowat · Mr David I Muir · Mr & Mrs W J I Muir · Mr R M Muir-Simpson ca
Miss Sophia Muirhead · Mr D Munro · Miss E Munro · Eleanor E Munro
Mr Kenneth A Munro · Miss Hope Murdoch · Mrs J Murdoch
Mr John Murdoch · Agnes L Murray · Miss Eleanor V de B Murray
Provost George Murray jp · Miss Milly W Murray · Mr Peter S Murray
Miss Elizabeth Newlands lram · Mrs W Nichol · Miss F M Nicholson
Sir Iain Noble bt · Mrs Margaret Noble · Jean & Chris O'Hara
Mr J W Ollason · Mrs Maureen A Paisley · Mr Peter C Paisley
Miss W Park · Mr George C Parker ca · Mr Iain Paterson
Mrs J Paterson · Mrs J Paterson · Mrs Anwyn S Paton · Mrs A W Pattison
Mr Robert P Pattman · Mr Robert A Peacock ca · Mrs Joan Peat
Mrs Margaret Perratt · Mrs Irene P Philips · Mr W L Pilkington
Mrs E Pinkerton · Mr & Mrs Ian Pirrie · Miss M Pirrie
Mr William Dudgeon Praties · Mr Andrew H Primrose · Miss Pritchard
Mr William Sandeman Quaile · Mr Dominic Quigley
Mr & Mrs M B Randalls · Dr & Mrs H A Rankin · Miss Mary E Rankin
Prof & Mrs R A Rankin · Mrs Jean M M Reid · Mr & Mrs W Rennie
Mr Ian N Reynard · Mr & Mrs H Richardson · Mr & Mrs David M Richmond
Dr Ian D Riley md · Mrs J Rintoul · Mr P Rintoul · Mr Ingram Ritchie
Mrs Margaret Robb · Mrs A Robertson · Miss Elizabeth Robertson
Miss L E Robertson · Miss M Robertson · Mr & Mrs A Robinson
Mr David A Roser · Mr George A Roser · Mrs Helen M Ross · Mrs A Rouse

Miss M Rule · Mr H L I Runciman · Mrs Maureen Russell
Mrs Thelma Sanjana · Mrs Hilda E Sayers · Mr T Schuster-Davis
Mr John D Scobie · Mr & Mrs Charles M Scott · Mr & Mrs John K Scott
Mrs M Scott · Mr R F Scott · Miss Susan Scott · Mrs June Scouler
Rev Dr Henry R Sefton · Mr David Selbie · Mr A Graham Service
Dr John Shaw-Dunn · Miss E Sheret · Miss Mary C Sheridon · Mr D Siddons
Mr & Mrs E Sim · Mrs Rosina H Sinclair · Sir Andrew Sloan qpm ba
Mr John Sloane · Mr I B Smail bsc · Mr & Mrs Hunter Smart · Miss E A Smith
Mr J Ross Smith · Miss Jennie B F Smith · Miss M F Smith
Mrs Muriel K A Smith · Dr Rosemary Smith · Mrs Agnes C Sneddon
Mr John B Somerville · Elizabeth Sommerfield · Miss A Anne Sommerville
Mrs Frances G Sommerville · Miss F M Spiers · Miss C & Miss M McP Steen
Mr Maurice Steuart-Corry · Miss C Stewart · Miss I G Stewart
The Very Rev Professor James S Stewart dd · Miss Karen Stewart
Mr & Mrs T N Stewart · Mrs Margaret M Stobie · Mr R Strachan
Mr R C Struthers · Mrs Harriet Sutherland · Dr Hugh Sutherland
Mr Stewart Sutherland · Mrs M V Sweet
Mr Andrew L Tannahill ostj ceng mimeche · Mr & Mrs J Taylor
Mrs Janet Taylor · Mr & Mrs M Taylor · Dr & Mrs Phillips Teo
Mrs Zora R Third · Mr Ian Thom · Sir Patrick M Thomas dso td lld dl ma
Dr & Mrs John Thomson · Mr Oliver C W Thomson · Mrs C Thompson
Mrs Valerie M Trotter · Mr John R Turner · Mr L M Vaughan · Mr W Waite
Dr & Mrs D Wakeford · Mr A G O Walker · Dr Anne M Z Walker
Mrs Muriel A A Walker · Mr J Walker · Miss Joan N Wallace
The Lord Wallace of Campsie kstj dl ssc · Mrs M Warden
Mr Ian Wardlaw · Mrs A Weir · Miss E L S Weir · Mr William R Weir
Mr Malcolm Wilkie · Miss C Wilson · Miss M Wilson · Mrs E Winchester
Dr M Woods · Miss Alexandrina Wotherspoon · Miss Agnes Wright
Mr & Mrs Wyper and Family · Sir Eric Yarrow
Alexander H & Sheena Young · Mr Richard M Young · Mrs W Zahra

List compiled by The Society of Friends of Glasgow Cathedral